The Adventures of
Pirate

"Pirate In The Dock"

By Janul

My name is Pirate, come with me
And see my life afloat
I'm not a ship that sails the sea
I am a narrowboat

----

www.JanulPublications.co.uk

Published by Janul Publications

The Accident

'Twas in the bleak midwinter
When icy winds were blowing
The water it began to freeze
Canals were stopped from flowing

Pirate sat beside the bank
All snug and warm inside
But no-one could anticipate
The problems he would hide

He kept things very secret
So quietly he was moored
& no-one saw the accident
'Till water round him thawed

The levels of the deep canal
Had dropped so very low
His bottom sat upon the ground
As water ceased to flow

Pirate's rear was grounded
How much he couldn't tell
His rudder hurt, it wouldn't move
He didn't feel too well

Help was needed swiftly
And soon it did arrive
The Doctor stood and shook his head
Would Pirate now survive?

"We'll need to do things quickly"
The Doc rolled up his sleeves
& into icy water plunged his arms
Through mud and leaves

He quickly found the problem
A dislocated rudder
"He's got to go to hospital"
Poor Pirate felt a shudder

Pirate wasn't happy
He didn't feel prepared
The big boat felt so very small
In fact he was quite scared

How were they going to move him
He couldn't steer the way
With a rudder that was broken?
Oh, this was an awful day

The Doctor had the answer
"To hospital you'll go
We'll fetch The Duke, your friend
He'll help by giving you a tow"

"But Duke is only little
Too small for towing me"
Poor Pirate felt like crying, but
The Doctor said "We'll see

Let's go & get The Duke, we'll ask
If he is feeling strong
I'm sure that he'll work very hard
At pulling you along

He'll want to help me save you
& if The Duke will steer
Your engine can help him along
Be brave, you mustn't fear"

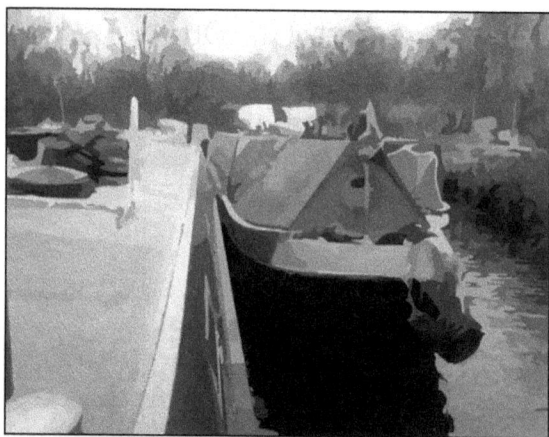

So Pirate waited patiently
In icy wind and rain
Trying to be very brave
& not to show his pain

He really did feel very ill
So scared his life was ended
But look – here comes The Duke
To take poor Pirate to be mended!

Duke The Hero

Duke came rushing to his pal
With Pirate's worried crew
"Oh no, what an emergency
Just tell me what to do!"

He snuggled up to Pirate's side
Gave comfort to his friend
& ropes were tied between the boats
Now joined from end to end

The space was tight to get them out
The crew was short of luck
Ropes & poles were pushed & pulled
But Pirate he got stuck

Every time poor Duke was steered
The wind it blew them back
"Come on" said Duke, "hold on there
& together we'll attack!"

Pirate took the deepest breath
So full of pain & strife
& with a noise so full of fear
His engine came to life

So Duke he steered & Pirate pushed
Two engines worked as one
To pull them clear & on their way
Together, they were gone

The journey it was very slow
The weather cold & raining
But little Duke he battled on
The ropes between them straining

On they went & through the lock
(The way they'd been before)
& every time they'd done a mile
They found there were some more

For hours they did battle on
With Pirate's growing plight
Then suddenly the Doctor said
"The hospital's in sight"

They turned towards familiar gates
That looked just like a lock
But here it was, the "Rudder Ward"
They called it a "dry dock"

Pirate looked quite worried
He stayed close to his friend
Beyond the gates what happens next
& is it a dead end?

The ropes were taken from him
That tied their sides together
The lock gates opened wide
- Would Pirate be in there forever?

They pulled him in quite swiftly
With ropes, it took some skill
To get him in the tiny space
Poor Pirate felt quite ill

Duke was not allowed as well
He had to stay outside
"Don't worry mate, I'll visit you!"
-   Poor Pirate almost cried

As Duke was quickly moved away
A little tug appeared
Pulling in "Geronimo"
- & nearly dead, they feared

"Oh dear" thought Pirate "look at him
It's very hard to tell
If he will live, he's worse than me
He makes me look quite well!"

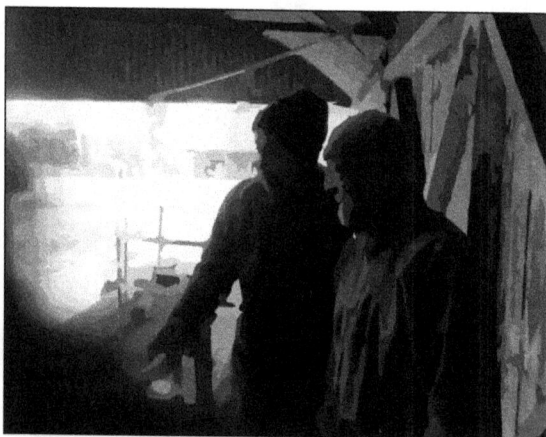

Doctors stood & shook their heads
The gates were closed behind
Getting through this crisis point
Was clearly now in mind

They signalled then to close the gate
"Move quickly!" came the shout
And fearing for the narrowboats
They pumped the water out

The Operation

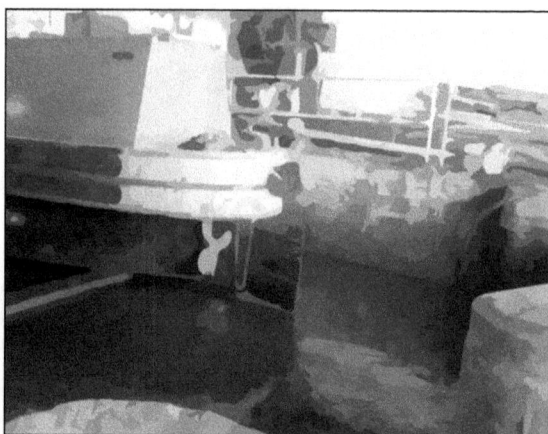

Pirate was now really scared
The water was descending
He was a boat, designed to float
Did this mean life was ending?

The water fell & down and down
They settled, well supported
On massive blocks of aged wood
- Some of his fears were thwarted

Gradually the water drained
The dock became quite dry
The Doctor now could walk around
-   To fix the boats he'd try

He now could see their undersides
To find what they had broken
The crew & Pirate held their breath
& not a word was spoken

"We're going to have to operate"
The Doctor said at last
"I think that Pirate's going to live
If we can get there fast

Geronimo I'm not so sure
It's serious through & through
He's going to need a welder
Yes, that's what we'll have to do"

"Geronimo, are you OK"
Said Pirate, feeling stronger
"You're not alone, I'm here for you
This pain can't last much longer

Oh dear, they're going to fix me now
Let's hope it's fairly quick"
Geronimo did not reply
He really did feel sick

The Doctor sighed & set to work
He tried to hide a shudder
The shaft had popped out of the cup
On Pirate's damaged rudder

With heated cries of "lift it up" &
"Drop it into place"
The shaft dropped back into the hole
- the rudder moved with grace

Pirate felt much better now
His tiller moved with ease
But then he saw Geronimo
"Oh my! – Do save him PLEASE!"

So time to fix Geronimo
The operation started
A welder swiftly made a seam
Right where the join had parted

For a moment, breaths were held
Until the weld had cooled
Geronimo, his tiller moved
- He'd really had them fooled

So both the boats were well enough
To swim in water deep
But the Doctor gave his orders now
- "It's time you got some sleep!

I know you're feeling better
But you can't go out until
I'm satisfied you're really well
You've both been very ill"

The boats got quite excited
They knew they soon would roam
But soon they were both fast asleep
With dreams of going home

Going Home

The sun it rose so bright & new
The friends were feeling well
(From swapping stories all night long
But this we must not tell)

The Doctor came & saw the friends
To send them on their way
"You've both recovered very well
& can go home today"

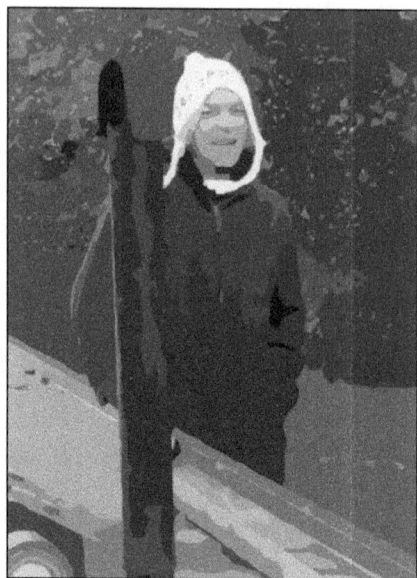

The crews arrived with happy smiles
Well rested from the night
They'd really felt exhausted
After witnessing the plight

The water flooded in & Pirate
Soon forgot his fears
He said "I feel so well
I haven't felt this good in years"

Pirate backed out slowly
& feeling very small
He moored beside a widebeam barge
Which was so big and tall

"How are you feeling little tug?"
The bigger boat did say
"I feared we'd never pull you through
But now you're on your way"

"Thank you Ma'am, I'm better now"
Said Pirate as he waited
Geronimo was backing out
& both felt quite elated

So glad to see his new found pal
Was clearly on the mend
Pirate hoped Geronimo
Would always be his friend

Pirate felt quite fortunate
That such a friend he'd met
They'd stuck together, thick & thin
& never would forget

But now 'twas time to say "Goodbye"
& go their separate ways
Many journeys still to come
For many, many days

Geronimo he gave a wave
& Pirate looked ahead
It really was so very sad
No words left to be said

But Pirate motored onwards
So happy he'd recovered
& soon there was a nice surprise
Just waiting to be discovered

For as he did approach a lock
So big and tall and gated
Pirate wore a beaming smile
-   Just look, The Duke, had waited!

Anxious now for Pirate's health
Duke waited for his friend
This wasn't time to leave him
& he'd stay until the end

"Nice to see you", shouted Duke
"You took your time, I fear
But now it's time for going home
So come on, over here!"

Pirate soon got going
(He now felt very well)
- Of doctors & Geronimo
He'd lots of tales to tell

The old friends chatted as they went
& Duke he learnt a lot
About the dry dock hospital
& treatment that you got

Some day they'll meet Geronimo
When on their way they roam
- But today, our Pirate's very glad
He's fixed .... & going home!

Dedicated to "The Crimson Pirate" & Warren

Acknowledgements to:

- The Duke, for being a Hero & my Friend
- Dave Handley for sending Duke as an Ambulance Man
- Geronimo (& Coco for her permission to use his photos)
- Uxbridge Boat Centre, especially to Alan for allowing the photoshoot
- Brian Hansell, 1st Engineer & oil can man

www.theadventuresofpirate.co.uk
pirate@theadventuresofpirate.co.uk

www.ingramcontent.com/pod-product-compliance
Lightning Source LLC
Chambersburg PA
CBHW071841020426
42331CB00007B/1809